C000245977

Si

by Iain Gray

Lang**Syne**

PUBLISHING

WRITING *to* REMEMBER

Lang**Syne**

PUBLISHING

WRITING *to* REMEMBER

79 Main Street, Newtongrange,
Midlothian EH22 4NA
Tel: 0131 344 0414   Fax: 0845 075 6085
E-mail: info@lang-syne.co.uk
www.langsyneshop.co.uk

Design by Dorothy Meikle
Printed by Printwell Ltd
© Lang Syne Publishers Ltd 2020

ISBN 978-1-85217-117-9

Sinclair

SEPT NAMES INCLUDE:

Caird
Clouston
Clyne
Linklater
Lyall
Mason

Sinclair

MOTTO:
Commit thy work to God.

CREST:
A cockerel.

TERRITORY:
Midlothian, Caithness, Orkney.

Chapter one:

The origins of the clan system

by Rennie McOwan

The original Scottish clans of the Highlands and the great families of the Lowlands and Borders were gatherings of families, relatives, allies and neighbours for mutual protection against rivals or invaders.

Scotland experienced invasion from the Vikings, the Romans and English armies from the south. The Norman invasion of what is now England also had an influence on land-holding in Scotland. Some of these invaders stayed on and in time became 'Scottish'.

The word clan derives from the Gaelic language term 'clann', meaning children, and it was first used many centuries ago as communities were formed around tribal lands in glens and mountain fastnesses.

The format of clans changed over the centuries, but at its best the chief and his family held the land on behalf of all, like trustees, and the ordinary clansmen and women believed they had a blood relationship with the founder of their clan.

There were two way duties and obligations. An inadequate chief could be deposed and replaced by someone of greater ability.

Clan people had an immense pride in race. Their relationship with the chief was like adult children to a father and they had a real dignity.

The concept of clanship is very old and a more feudal notion of authority gradually crept in.

Pictland, for instance, was divided into seven principalities ruled by feudal leaders who were the strongest and most charismatic leaders of their particular groups.

By the sixth century the 'British' kingdoms of Strathclyde, Lothian and Celtic Dalriada (Argyll) had emerged and Scotland, as one nation, began to take shape in the time of King Kenneth MacAlpin.

Some chiefs claimed descent from

ancient kings which may not have been accurate in every case.

By the twelfth and thirteenth centuries the clans and families were more strongly brought under the central control of Scottish monarchs.

Lands were awarded and administered more and more under royal favour, yet the power of the area clan chiefs was still very great.

The long wars to ensure Scotland's independence against the expansionist ideas of English monarchs extended the influence of some clans and reduced the lands of others.

Those who supported Scotland's greatest king, Robert the Bruce, were awarded the territories of the families who had opposed his claim to the Scottish throne.

In the Scottish Borders country – the notorious Debatable Lands – the great families built up a ferocious reputation for providing warlike men accustomed to raiding into England and occasionally fighting one another.

Chiefs had the power to dispense justice and to confiscate lands and clan warfare produced a society where martial virtues – courage, hardiness, tenacity – were greatly admired.

Gradually the relationship between the clans and the Crown became strained as Scottish monarchs became more orientated to life in the Lowlands and, on occasion, towards England.

The Highland clans spoke a different language, Gaelic, whereas the language of Lowland Scotland and the court was Scots and in more modern times, English.

Highlanders dressed differently, had different customs, and their wild mountain land sometimes seemed almost foreign to people living in the Lowlands.

It must be emphasised that Gaelic culture was very rich and story-telling, poetry, piping, the clarsach (harp) and other music all flourished and were greatly respected.

Highland culture was different from other parts of Scotland but it was not inferior or less sophisticated.

Central Government, whether in London or Edinburgh, sometimes saw the Gaelic clans as

*"The spirit of the clan means much
to thousands of people"*

a challenge to their authority and some sent expeditions into the Highlands and west to crush the power of the Lords of the Isles.

Nevertheless, when the eighteenth century Jacobite Risings came along the cause of the Stuarts was mainly supported by Highland clans.

The word Jacobite comes from the Latin for James – Jacobus. The Jacobites wanted to restore the exiled Stuarts to the throne of Britain.

The monarchies of Scotland and England became one in 1603 when King James VI of Scotland (1st of England) gained the English throne after Queen Elizabeth died.

The Union of Parliaments of Scotland and England, the Treaty of Union, took place in 1707.

Some Highland clans, of course, and Lowland families opposed the Jacobites and supported the incoming Hanoverians.

After the Jacobite cause finally went down at Culloden in 1746 a kind of ethnic cleansing took place. The power of the chiefs was curtailed. Tartan and the pipes were banned in law.

Many emigrated, some because they

wanted to, some because they were evicted by force. In addition, many Highlanders left for the cities of the south to seek work.

Many of the clan lands became home to sheep and deer shooting estates.

But the warlike traditions of the clans and the great Lowland and Border families lived on, with their descendants fighting bravely for freedom in two world wars.

Remember the men from whence you came, says the Gaelic proverb, and to that could be added the role of many heroic women.

The spirit of the clan, of having roots, whether Highland or Lowland, means much to thousands of people.

Chapter two:

Raiders from the north

Proud of a genealogy that can be traced back to at least the ninth century, the Sinclairs have not only played a prominent role in Scotland's turbulent history, but are reputed to be the custodians of a secret tradition stretching back to the time of Jesus.

Their roots lie in distant Norway, from where they embarked in their longships to raid, ravage, and pillage before settling in what became known as Norse-man's-land, better known as Normandy, in France.

By 912 they had risen to great power and influence, owning vast tracts of land and mighty strongholds. A force to be reckoned with, their leader, Rollo, signed a treaty with Charles III of France that created him Count of Rouen.

The treaty was signed at the castle of St Clair-sur-Epte, named after a hermit, and it was from this location that they took the name

St. Clair, more popularly recognised today as Sinclair, and reckoned to be one of the oldest surnames in Europe.

Nine Sinclair knights fought with great distinction on the side of their fellow Norman, William the Conqueror, at the Battle of Hastings in 1066, a battle that paved the way for the Norman supremacy in England, and it was either one of these knights, or a relative, who later settled in Scotland.

A Henry Sinclair is recorded as holding lands in Lothian in 1162, while Sir William Sinclair, a guardian of the young Alexander III,

was granted the barony of Rosslyn, in Midlothian, in 1280.

The Sinclairs had obviously inherited the martial prowess of their descendants who had fought at Hastings, for in 1303, Sir Henry Sinclair was one of the Scottish commanders at the bloody Battle of Roslin fought on his own lands of Rosslyn between a force of 30,000 and only 8,000 Scots.

Despite the overwhelming odds against them, the Scots won the day. Old place names in the area are reminders of the battle.

There is 'Shin-banes Field', where hundreds of bones were uncovered years after the battle, and the 'Stinking Rig', where, according to one chronicler 'multitudes of the slain were buried, and, not being sufficiently covered, emitted an intolerable stench'.

There is also the 'Killburn', a brook that was said to have been discoloured with blood for three days after the battle.

Sir Henry also fought in the cause of Scotland's freedom eleven years later at the

Battle of Bannockburn. He was also one of the signatories of the famous Declaration of Arbroath of 1320, while his brother William, Bishop of Dunkeld, led an army that repulsed a force of English at Donibristle in 1317.

Two of Sir Henry's sons, William and John, were among the knights who accompanied Sir James Douglas on a mission in 1330 to bury the heart of the great warrior king Robert the Bruce in the Holy Land.

Attacked by Moors while travelling through Spain, Lord James and the two Sinclair brothers were killed, but the heart of Bruce was returned to Scotland and buried in the grounds of Melrose Abbey, in the Borders.

A grandson of Sir Henry is recognised as having laid the foundation for the Sinclairs' great territories in the distant northern realms of Scotland, through his marriage to Isabella, Countess of Orkney, while one of his descendants, also named Henry, inherited the title of Earl of Orkney in 1379.

Known as the Prince of Orkney, the

The Norsemen in their longships

blood of his seafaring Norse ancestors coursed strongly through his veins. He conquered the Faroe Islands in 1391, gained control of Shetland, and in 1398 embarked on a remarkable voyage across the Atlantic in a fleet of twelve ships, along with the Venetian navigator Antonio Zeno.

A rare chart known as the Zeno Map, in addition to archaeological finds, reveals that they explored modern day Labrador, Nova Scotia, and Massachusetts, indicating that a Sinclair was responsible for discovering America a century before Columbus.

The northern power of the Sinclairs was increased in 1455 when King James II granted William, the third Sinclair Earl of Orkney, the earldom of Caithness. The Earl of Caithness is recognised to this day as chief of the Clan Sinclair.

The Sinclairs lost the earldom of Orkney in 1470 when they were forced to 'resign' it to James III in exchange for Ravenscraig Castle, in Fife.

Chapter three:

Secret of
the Holy Grail

Standing on the edge of the scenic Esk Valley near the village of Roslin, in Midlothian, and attracting thousands of visitors every year is the mysterious Rosslyn Chapel, built in 1446 by William Sinclair, who was created Lord Sinclair in 1449.

Founded as a collegiate church and consecrated to St Matthew it is thought to encode in stone a mystery that links a band of warrior monks who were known as the Knights Templar, the origins of Scottish Freemasonry, and a secret relating to the Holy Grail.

It had been intended that the chapel be built in the form of a cross, with a tower in the centre - but it was never completed. Only the east transept and the choir were built.

Built in a style described as 'florid

Gothic', it is famous for its Apprentice's Pillar, which stands in the south-east corner.

Decorated with four wreaths of flowers, spiralling from base to crown, it is the subject of a curious legend – that the Master Mason, jealous of the skill of a young apprentice who sculpted the pillar, killed him with a blow to the forehead.

With strange echoes of Freemasonic legend, three stone heads at the west of the chapel commemorate this slaying.

One is thought to be the apprentice's mother, and is known as The Widowed Mother, while one depicts the apprentice with a gash above his right eye, and the other depicts the Master Mason.

This is taken as evidence that the masons who built the chapel were privy to esoteric knowledge that had been transmitted to them through those Knights Templar who had sought refuge in Scotland after being outlawed by Papal Bull in 1307.

The Templars, who had been formed in 1118 to guard the pilgrim routes to the Holy

Land, are thought to have excavated the ruins of Solomon's Temple in Jerusalem, and unearthed an awesome secret relating to Christianity.

Some claim the secret may have been in the form of ancient parchments – or even the famed Holy Grail of the Last Supper itself. Another theory is that the grail may not be an actual vessel, or cup, but a secret relating to the bloodline of Christ.

A persistent claim is that a body of refugee Templars fought on the side of Robert the Bruce at Bannockburn, and that their secret knowledge was later transmitted, through what became Scottish Freemasonry, to some of Scotland's noblest families, including the Sinclairs.

Sir William Sinclair, some believe, may actually have built Rosslyn Chapel as a repository for the secrets of the Templars.

Twelve Sinclair barons are known to be buried in sealed vaults beneath the chapel, laid to rest in full armour. Who knows what else may lie gathering the dust of centuries in these sealed vaults.

There is also a legend that was familiar to Sir Walter Scott. In *The Lay of the Last Minstrel*, he wrote of how on the eve of a Sinclair's death a lurid red light fills the chapel.

There is a tradition that, in 1441, James II had appointed a Sinclair of Rosslyn as Patron and Protector of Scottish Masons, and that the office was hereditary.

In 1628 a charter was drawn up by William Schaw, Master of Works to James VI that sought to obtain from the king the right of the Sinclairs to be recognised as having jurisdiction over masons as patrons and judges.

The Charter argued that it had been recognised from age to age that the lairds of Roslin had been patrons and protectors of the Craft and its privileges, and that this had 'died out through neglect'.

The attempt to gain royal patronage failed, however. What may have hindered the attempt was that at this period the Roman

Catholic William Sinclair was in such trouble with his local presbytery for his persistent 'lewd' behaviour that he was forced to retire to Ireland.

In 1736, however, it was a Sinclair of Rosslyn who was appointed the first Grand Master of the Grand Lodge of Scotland – after having renounced his hereditary claims to the title.

The Sinclairs had never been able to furnish proof that they had been granted the hereditary title of patron and protector of masons, and there is a possibility that the original charters granting this privilege may either have been destroyed by fire or pillaged by Cromwell's troops in 1650 when they attacked Roslin Castle.

The Sinclairs of the West of Scotland, particularly in Argyllshire, provide a possible curious link to the Sinclairs of Rosslyn and their connection to Freemasonry.

Their Gaelic name is Clann-na-Cearda – Children of the Craft, or Craftsmen. 'Craftsman' is thought to refer to a goldsmith or tinsmith, but it is possible it may also refer to the 'Craft' of Masonry.

One of the Sinclair sept names, meanwhile, is 'Mason', as is 'Caird', from the Gaelic 'Ceard'.

Chapter four:

On the field of battle

The 16th, 17th, and 18th centuries saw the Sinclairs at war on many fronts, including on occasion with one another.

William Sinclair was one of the twelve Earls who fell with his king, James IV, at the disastrous Battle of Flodden in 1513.

So great was the slaughter among the Sinclairs of Caithness that to this day there is a tradition they have an aversion to wearing the colour green or crossing over the Ord Hill on a Monday – because it was on a Monday, clothed in green, that they marched over the Ord Hill on their way to Flodden Field.

Sixteen years later, in 1529, John, the third Earl of Caithness, attempted to regain his grandfather's Earldom of Orkney. It ended in disaster when the Earl was killed in a naval battle along with about 500 of his followers.

In 1542 it was largely due to the inept

leadership of Oliver Sinclair that an army of Scots was defeated at the Battle of Solway Moss.

The main seat of the Sinclair Earls of Caithness was the brooding Girnigoe Castle, on the rocky Caithness coastline.

It was in Girnigoe's deep and dank dungeon that in 1571 the Earl imprisoned his son and heir, John, who strangled his brother, William, with his chains before dying from thirst.

It was through William, however, that the Sinclairs of Ulbster, in Caithness, were founded.

A renowned member of this family was Sir John Sinclair (1754-1835), first Baronet of Ulbster, who was editor of The First Statistical Account of Scotland, and is also recognised as a pioneering agricultural improver, founding a Board of Agriculture for Scotland in 1793.

In August of 1612, in what became known as the Sinclair Raid, George Sinclair, a nephew of the Earl of Caithness, was involved in one of the most decisive defeats inflicted on a Scottish army on foreign soil in a single encounter.

A force of 300 Scottish troops under
Colonel Andrew Ramsay and Captain Sinclair
were ambushed and attacked by a peasant
army while making their perilous way through

the Gulbrandsdalen Valley, in Norway, while en route to join the forces of the King of Sweden, who was at war with Denmark.

Captain Sinclair, riding a white horse, made for an easy target, and he is said to have been shot through the heart by a bullet in the form of a silver button - the peasants believing that Scottish officers wore charms which protected them from lead and steel bullets.

Only 134 Scots survived the ambush, but 120 of them were later massacred after being taken prisoner. The incident is remembered to this day in Norwegian ballads, while the site of the ambush is known as Sinklair Dokka, or Sinclair Dip.

The son of the 10th Lord Sinclair, known to history as the famous Master of Sinclair, was sentenced to death in 1708 while serving with Marlborough in Flanders for shooting a fellow officer to death.

He made for the safety of Prussia, but returned to Scotland after being pardoned four years later.

The Sinclairs had always been renowned for their adherence to the cause of the Royal House of Stuart, and the Master of Sinclair rallied to their cause during the 1715 Rebellion, leading a daring and successful raid off Burntisland to capture a ship containing a valuable supply of government munitions.

The Sinclairs raised 1,000 men to aid the cause of Charles Edward Stuart during the rebellion of 1745. Five hundred of them had been on their way to join the ill-fated prince, but disbanded when they heard his forces had been routed at Culloden.

Off the field of battle, other noted Sinclairs have included George Sinclair, the author and professor of practical philosophy at Glasgow University who superintended the laying of Edinburgh's water pipes in 1673, and James Sinclair (1824-81), who patented inventions which include a loom, a steam carriage, and gravitating compass.

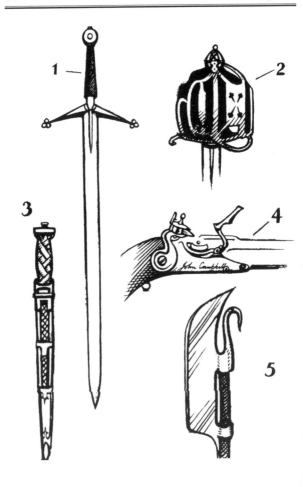

Clan weapons

1) The claymore or two-handed sword
   (fifteenth or early sixteenth century)

2) Basket hilt of broadsword
   made in Stirling, 1716

3) Highland dirk
   (eighteenth century)

4) Steel pistol *(detail)* made in Doune

5) Head of Lochaber Axe as carried
   in the '45 and earlier